LOVE U

DRAWING BOOK

This book belongs to:

____

89340799R00063

Made in the USA
Columbia, SC
13 February 2018